# NO TRUTH WITHOUT RUTH

THE LIFE OF
RUTH BADER
GINSBURG

By Kathleen Krull    Illustrated by Nancy Zhang

HARPER
*An Imprint of HarperCollinsPublishers*

Library of Congress Control Number: 2017932855
ISBN 978-0-06-256011-7

The artist used traditional arts media and digital techniques
to make the illustrations for this book.
Typography by Rachel Zegar

17    18    19    20    21    SCP    10    9    8    7    6    5    4    3    2    1

❖

First Edition

To Dr. Virginia Loh-Hagan, shrewd judge of

pianos and so much more

—K.K.

To all the women who are chasing their dreams

—N.Z.

Ida B. Wells

Alice Paul

Virginia Woolf

Susan B. Anthony

We may take it for granted now that women should be treated as equals, that daughters are valued just as much as sons. But girls and women used to face unfairness every day—in their families, schools, and workplaces.

Sometimes the things we take for granted today happened because of a single person. This is the story of one of those change-makers:

**Ruth Bader Ginsburg, fierce fighter for fairness and truth.**

RUTH BADER GINSBURG

Ruth always said that her mother, Celia, was the smartest person she ever knew.

Celia loved to learn. She brought home straight-A report cards and showed them to her father. He didn't care about that—because she was a girl.

## That was the way things were then.

When Celia was fifteen, she graduated high school three years early, at the top of her class. She went to work in a factory to earn the money to send her older brother on to college. After she got married, she quit her job, because wives weren't supposed to work outside the home.

Celia poured her love of learning into her daughter. Every week the two of them walked to the library, where Celia pushed Ruth from Greek myths to Nancy Drew and beyond. The library was right above a Chinese restaurant, so from then on reading made Ruth think of savory smells—and her mom. She was hungry for knowledge, always wanting to find the truth.

## No truth without Ruth!

Ruth's parents and grandparents were Jewish immigrants who fled religious persecution in Russia and Poland. Their neighborhood in Brooklyn was home to many new Americans. They worked toward a better life, dreaming that their sons would become doctors and lawyers. Then their daughters would marry them. Girls were not considered equal to boys and were not expected to have careers.

But Celia's dream was for her daughter to be important in her own right, just as valued as a son.

Once Ruth brought home a less-than-perfect report card, and she could see her mom's disappointment. She got the message.

*Her mom expected great things of her.*

A-

When Ruth was thirteen, at her Jewish summer camp, she was the "camp rabbi," the leader of religious services—decades before women were allowed to become real rabbis.

That was the year World War II ended, and Ruth was painfully aware of her own relatives among the millions killed in Europe because they were Jewish. There was unfairness in America too—Ruth sometimes saw signs that read "No dogs or Jews allowed."

In high school, besides earning straight As, she threw herself into activities. Girls weren't encouraged to play sports then. As the leader of the Go-Getters, a pep club that cheered the athletes, she twirled her baton with such energy that one day she chipped her tooth.

But Ruth had a sad secret at home. Her mother was fighting cancer. Ruth did her homework sitting by Celia's bed because she knew how much her mom loved to see her study.

Celia died the night before Ruth's graduation. Instead of speaking in front of the school that day and accepting her academic awards, Ruth helped her father make funeral arrangements. The Jewish mourning service required ten men.

## Ruth wasn't allowed to be part of the tradition.

Losing her mom so early in her life was a terrible blow.

Carrying out her mom's dream became Ruth's goal. That fall she enrolled at college. Her grades were so stellar that she'd won a scholarship—plus Celia had put some money away for her.

In college, other students called her "scary smart," because it was a time when girls were supposed to hide their smarts. Ruth memorized the locations of the women's bathrooms on campus and hid out, studying there.

She read in the news about Joseph McCarthy, a famous senator from Wisconsin who attacked people he thought were national enemies. He ruined lives and threatened America's freedoms. Ruth was impressed by the brave lawyers who stood up to him.

*Being a lawyer— a fighter for fairness— seemed heroic.*

Most young men didn't care if a girl had a brain. The first one who did was Martin. Ruth married him, and they journeyed toward becoming young lawyers together.

In law school, Ruth stood out in a major way. She was one of only nine women in her class of more than five hundred.

Most places around campus were opening up to women, but a few were still men-only. Professors who weren't comfortable with women students sometimes called on them as a joke, to mock them if they didn't know the right answers.

One evening, the dean of the law school invited the nine female students to dinner at his house. How thoughtful. But it turned out he wanted to ask why each was there taking the place of a man.

Ruth was so flustered that she mumbled something she knew he'd like: she wanted to understand her husband's work better.

Late one night, for an assignment, she *had* to get a law journal from the room in the library where the old magazines were kept. But that room was still closed to women. She begged the guard to at least bring the magazine to her outside, but he refused. She had to find another way to complete her assignment, keeping her perfect grades intact.

Outside of class, some men called her "Ruthless Ruthie" and even worse names.

She decided those names were better than being called "mouse."

## Ruth was becoming a warrior.

She graduated at the very top of her class. Her mom would have been so proud.

But she didn't get a single job offer. Every law firm rejected her. Job descriptions said "Men Only."

A kindly professor helped, trying to find her a job as a clerk to a judge instead. One judge asked if Ruth wore skirts—he couldn't stand women who wore pants. Then the judge said never mind: "I'm not hiring a woman."

Ruth began clerking for another judge. From there she went on to teach law, as a professor at one of the few law schools willing to hire women.

And one day, Ruth Bader Ginsburg began

*to fight for the truth,*
*to fight to*
*change America.*

Her students planted the seed. As the years passed, there were more women in law school—about six for every hundred men. One day some of them asked Ruth to teach a new course: "Women and the Law."

She hit the library to read everything available. It didn't take much time. Hardly anything had been written about this topic.

What she found was that laws about women were unfair. The legal system seemed based on old-fashioned ideas about women being different from men—and not in a good way. It struck Ruth that whenever the law used the word "protection"—as in women needing special protection—it meant the slamming of a door.

But it was the 1970s, and women's roles in society were changing.

Ruth asked herself:
How could the law catch up?

She divided her time between teaching and helping to found the
Women's Rights Project. This was a group of lawyers who fought for
women fired for being pregnant, girls not allowed to participate in sports,
and men denied time off for child care and against the endless unfair rules
about hiring women and promoting them at work.

Ruth was the group's chief lawyer. She wrote arguments for many of its cases, sometimes going to the lower courts to argue them in person.

Some men called her "picky" and "demanding." And sometimes when she talked, she noticed that no one seemed to hear until a man said the same thing.

But she kept making her points,
a fierce fighter for fairness,
speaking up for the truth.

One January afternoon in 1972, she got ready to argue her first case in person in front of the mighty Supreme Court, the highest court of all.

These were the nine most important judges in the country, all men, appointed to the bench for life. They wore heavy black robes and sat up above the courtroom in high-backed chairs. As they made decisions on the most controversial cases of all, they asked lots of tough questions of the lawyers in front of them.

Ruth was prepared, but she was too nervous to eat lunch for fear of not keeping it down.

"Mr. Chief Justice, and may it please the Court," she started. She was queasy, her voice shaky. Thinking of her mom helped. For that very reason, she wore her mom's circle pin and her earrings. She was suiting up in armor to fight her opponent that day: the United States government. And truth was her weapon.

Ruth began by talking about an earlier case, of an Idaho mother not allowed to take care of her dead son's estate because she wasn't a man. Ruth knew the case well—she had written the argument that the mother should be allowed to handle her son's affairs, and her side had won. The Supreme Court had declared for the first time that a law treating men and women differently violated the United States Constitution—it was illegal.

## Now Ruth wanted to build on that decision.

In presenting that day's case, Ruth felt a surge of confidence. After all, these men might be scary, but they were there to listen to her. This was an opportunity to teach.

A woman officer in the United States Air Force was being denied medical and housing benefits for her husband. Male officers had no trouble getting these benefits for their wives. Ruth argued that laws treating men and women differently were unfair—meant to keep women in their place, a place unequal to men.

Then she looked directly at the nine men and concluded with the words of Sarah Grimké, a famous fighter for women's right to vote:

*"I ask no favor for [women].*
*All I ask of our [brothers]*
*is that they take their*
*feet off our necks.*
*Thank you."*

Stony silence from all nine justices.

It was most unusual that not one of them had interrupted Ruth with questions. The men stared at her. Were they stunned? Not listening? Offended? Asleep?

The justices had hardly any experience with legal arguments about women.

In his diary that night, one of them graded her performance: "C+. Very precise female."

But five months later, after debating Ruth's case and the others on their docket, the nine justices handed down their verdict.

The vote was eight to one in favor of Ruth. This was a landmark victory: women were people too.

*Ruth had fought for fairness and won.*

The more Ruth appeared at the Supreme Court—always wearing her mother's pin and earrings—the more respect the judges showed her. Over the next nine years she won five of the six cases she argued in person, and she wrote the arguments for dozens more that other Women's Rights Project lawyers argued.

Ruth loved to win. But Supreme Court rulings were bigger than that. Future court cases are supposed to follow them. With all her victories, Ruth wasn't just winning.

In fighting for fairness,

## she was actually changing the way the country treated women.

Ruth chose her cases by looking for ways that men were being hurt too.

## Unfairness, she said, "is bad for everyone; it's bad for men, it's bad for children."

Her favorite case was a man with a baby in his arms. His wife had died in childbirth. She had earned twice as much as he did. But because he was a man, her Social Security checks—which would have allowed him to devote himself to raising their infant son—were cut off.

Ruth argued on his behalf and won.

Her last case before the Court was challenging a Missouri law that made jury duty optional for women. To Ruth this said that *women* were optional—unnecessary to important government functions.

The Court agreed, and she won again.

## No truth without Ruth!

By 1980, Ruth was the single most important fighter for fairness—women's and men's—in American history. She was famous.

The president, Jimmy Carter, chose Ruth for the second most powerful court in the land, the United States Court of Appeals. Instead of being a lawyer, now she was a judge, the one who asks the lawyers a lot of tough questions. Her job was to hand down verdicts on all kinds of cases, making decisions according to the Constitution, not according to her personal feelings. It was another way for her to battle unfairness.

Thirteen years and many verdicts later came a beautiful sunny day in the White House Rose Garden. President Bill Clinton announced Ruth's nomination to the highest court of all. "I know well how the Supreme Court affects the lives of all Americans personally and deeply." He called her "one of our nation's best judges."

In accepting, Ruth wore her mother's pin and earrings to honor the woman "who was taken away from me much too soon." Some listeners cried as she went on. "I pray I may be all that she would have been had she lived in an age when women could aspire and achieve and daughters are cherished as much as sons." An age when things were more fair—an age Ruth had fought hard for.

On her first day on the Supreme Court, she put on her long black robe. Now *she* was one of those nine important people sitting in the high-backed chairs.

In her first hour, she asked seventeen questions of the lawyers arguing the case—more than some justices had asked in weeks.

Now that she was the second woman on the Court, it had to add a women's bathroom.

Ruth worked harder than ever, helping to decide one important case after another in all areas of the law.

One of her biggest victories against unfairness came in 1996. Hundreds of high school girls were trying to apply to the Virginia Military Institute, but it was all-male and determined to stay that way. Ruth argued that its policy reinforced stereotypes about "the way women are."

Most of the other justices agreed with her. The Court ordered that VMI had to start admitting women as cadets—a landmark, far-reaching decision.

## No truth without Ruth.

With eight other judges deciding on cases, Ruth didn't always get her way. Sometimes the bravest thing she could do was dissent, or disagree, with the majority. She used dissent to make her voice heard when she saw signs that the progress she fought for was slipping.

One decision that angered her came in 2007. An Alabama woman had sued her employer on finding out after twenty years on the job that she was being paid much less than men holding the same job. The Court ruled against her, saying too much time had passed for her to take legal action.

Ruth dissented so strongly that Congress later overruled the Court. In 2009, the first piece of legislation that President Barack Obama signed was the Fair Pay Act in honor of the woman who had sued, so that this wouldn't happen again.

**Ruth's dissent
had become the law.
No truth without Ruth!**

Over the years on the Supreme Court, she twirled her baton

and went parasailing,

white-water rafting,

horseback riding,

paddleboarding,

and water-skiing.

But mostly Ruth worked, sometimes all through the night. She remained a fierce voice in favor of fairness. The other justices called her "fearless."

The fight for women's equality continues, but the America Ruth and her mother grew up in no longer exists, thanks in part to her.

She is on record as saying she'd like to see *nine* women on the Supreme Court.

Until then, she is RBG—scary smart and fearless, picky and demanding, and a powerful fighter against unfairness.

## No truth without Ruth!

# Ruth Bader Ginsburg Timeline

**1933:** Born in Brooklyn, New York

**1950:** Graduates from James Madison High School

**1954:** Graduates at the top of her class from Cornell University with a bachelor's degree in government

**1954:** Marries Martin Ginsburg and has two children, Jane (born 1955) and James (born 1965)

**1956–1959:** Attends Harvard University Law School until transferring to Columbia University Law School, graduating at the top of her class

**1959–1961**: Law clerk for a judge in the Southern District of New York

**1963–1980**: Professor at Rutgers University Law School and Columbia Law School

**1970s:** Director of the Women's Rights Project for the American Civil Liberties Union

**1980:** Appointed by President Jimmy Carter to the Court of Appeals for the District of Columbia

**1993:** Appointed by President Bill Clinton as the second woman to join the Supreme Court, a lifetime appointment

# The American Federal Court System
## The Supreme Court

The final place to appeal a verdict from a lower court.
It accepts only about 150 of the 5,000 cases it is asked to review,
and its verdicts affect every American's daily life.

## Thirteen Regional Courts of Appeals
## (or Appellate Courts)

Where to go when you want to appeal, or protest,
the verdict from a lower, or district, court.

## Ninety-four District Courts in Fifty States

Where most court cases start.

# Top 10 Moments When Ruth Bader Ginsburg Fought for Fairness on the Supreme Court

*UNITED STATES V. VIRGINIA* (1996): RBG spoke for the majority in ordering the Virginia Military Institute to admit women cadets.

*BUSH V. GORE* (2000), resolving the disputed 2000 presidential election between George W. Bush and Al Gore, allowing Florida's vote count to stand, which made Bush the winner. RBG dissented, or opposed the decision, arguing that it should have been left to the state court.

*LEDBETTER V. GOODYEAR TIRE & RUBBER COMPANY* (2007), ruling that employees cannot sue for pay discrimination if their claim is more than 180 days old. RBG dissented so strongly that a later law—the Lilly Ledbetter Fair Pay Act, signed by President Obama in 2009—reversed the ruling.

*SAFFORD UNIFIED SCHOOL DISTRICT V. REDDING* (2009), ruling that the strip-search of an eighth-grade girl suspected of possessing drugs was unconstitutional. RBG pointed out that the other justices (all male at the time) had "never been a thirteen-year-old girl" and was able to make them see her point.

*CITIZENS UNITED V. FEDERAL ELECTION COMMISSION* (2010), ruling that corporations and organizations can spend as much money as they want to help political candidates win elections. One of the strongest voices against the corrupting influence of money in politics, RBG dissented, declaring later, "If there was one decision I would overrule, it would be *Citizens United*."

*WAL-MART STORES, INC. V. DUKES* (2011), ruling that a women's class action suit against Wal-Mart for pay discrimination could not proceed because the women didn't have enough in common to constitute a class. RBG dissented (of course).

*SHELBY COUNTY V. HOLDER* (2013), ruling parts of the 1965 Voting Rights Act that protected minorities from discrimination were unconstitutional. RBG dissented, declaring that throwing out such protection was like "throwing away your umbrella in a rainstorm because you are not getting wet."

*UNITED STATES V. WINDSOR* (2013), ruling that the federal government can recognize same-sex marriages even in states where they are illegal. RBG agreed, and that year became the first Supreme Court justice to officiate at a same-sex wedding.

*BURWELL V. HOBBY LOBBY STORES, INC.* (2014), ruling that family-run businesses can claim a religious exemption from laws if the laws contradict the family's religious beliefs. RBG dissented, declaring, "The Court, I fear, has ventured into a minefield."

*KING V. BURWELL* (2015), ruling the Affordable Care Act constitutional. RBG agreed, and the effect was to defend the government's authority to enact social-welfare legislation.

# Sources

Ayer, Eleanor H. *Ruth Bader Ginsburg: Fire and Steel on the Supreme Court*. New York: Dillon, 1994.

Carmon, Irin, and Shana Knizhnik. *Notorious RBG: The Life and Times of Ruth Bader Ginsburg*. New York: Morrow, 2015.

Coyle, Marcia. *The Roberts Court: The Struggle for the Constitution*. New York: Simon & Schuster, 2013.

Dodson, Scott, ed. *The Legacy of Ruth Bader Ginsburg*. Cambridge: Cambridge University Press, 2015.

Halberstam, Malvina. "Ruth Bader Ginsburg," *Jewish Women: A Comprehensive Historical Encyclopedia*, https://jwa.org/encyclopedia/article/ginsburg-ruth-bader.

Henry, Christopher E. *Ruth Bader Ginsburg*. New York: Franklin Watts, 1994.

Hirshman, Linda R. *Sisters in Law: How Sandra Day O'Connor and Ruth Bader Ginsburg Went to the Supreme Court and Changed the World*. New York: HarperCollins, 2015.

"The History of the ACLU Women's Rights Project," https://www.aclu.org/history-aclu-womens-rights-project.

Lamb, Brian, Susan Swain, and Mark Farkas, eds. *The Supreme Court: A C-SPAN Book Featuring the Justices in Their Own Words*. New York: Public Affairs, 2010.

Notorious RBG, http://notoriousrbg.tumblr.com.

"Ruth Bader Ginsburg," http://www.makers.com/ruth-bader-ginsburg.

Strebeigh, Fred. *Equal: Women Reshape American Law*. New York: Norton, 2009.

The Supreme Court Historical Society, http://supremecourthistory.org/index.html.

Supreme Court of the United States, http://www.supremecourt.gov/default.aspx.

Toobin, Jeffrey. "Heavyweight," *New Yorker*, March 11, 2013.